*Ampersand Revisited* **is an inverted** *Odyssey*, **etched in searing—downright entomological—precision.**

*Ampersand Revisited* tracks a father's retreat from occult ways of knowing through the wounded meshwork of the son's very grammar: it is a kind of Odyssey, inverted. Magical powers—ancient craftiness—might make the epic hero, but they are an impossible burden to live with in the Manichean, and very American, riddle that forges *Ampersand*'s poeisis. Crossed & re-crossed with sex & suicide, school & mystery school, *Ampersand Revisited* riddles the drama not so much of the father's departure, but of his return. It is the vivid, laconic gloss of the ravages of mystical knowing. The son seeks the father through literature and sex while the mother does her Penelope work—her oblivion and recollection—by taking up with her coke-dealing suitor. And somehow a boy becomes a man. *Ampersand Revisited* does not speak through a Homeric mouth, but instead, through the Mallarmean page: everything in it is marked, marled by textuality: "the vague, diacritical marks of used condoms"; "half-finished light like the burned church of an idea"; "the spent hexagram of cigarettes & withered latex"; or here, why not enjoy a sentence in its entirety: "The low afternoon light solders the sliding glass door into a stab of gold circuitry you step through, wincing, as you encounter the aphasic grammar of the falling snow."

Either language is the error out of which we proceed or the "warped platelet" through which Totality is given to us, and according to which we chart and gloss the intricate incommensurables that either corrupt or enlighten—but I should not say *or*. I should say &: "Perhaps the reason why I've loved the direct address all these years / is because you can / talk to the beloved & the reader / without each one really knowing / about the other."

*Ampersand Revisited* is a haunting, an original achievement: in its tenderness; in its exhausted, even sore limpidity, I find more & more surprises, more gifts. I have read it again & again.          **ARIANA REINES**

# AMPERSAND REVISITED

FENCE
BOOKS

# AMPERSAND REVISITED
# SIMEON BERRY

THE NATIONAL POETRY SERIES
SELECTED BY ARIANA REINES

Published in the United States by Fence Books, Science Library 320, University of
Albany, 1400 Washington Avenue, Albany, NY 12222

www.fenceportal.org

Fence Books are distributed by Consortium Book Sales & Distribution (cbsd.com) and
Small Press Distribution (spdbooks.org).

Cover photograph, *Rock Wall #2, West Hartford, CT*, 1959.
Photograph by Paul Caponigro ©1959
Cover and interior design by Jess Puglisi

Library of Congress Cataloging in Publication Data
Berry, Simeon [1973- ]
Ampersand Revisited / Simeon Berry

Library of Congress Control Number: 2015933581

ISBN-13 978-1-934200-92-6

FIRST EDITION
10 9 8 7 6 5 4 3 2

Fence Books are published in partnership with the University at Albany and the New
York State Writers Institute, and with help from the New York State Council on the Arts
and the National Endowment for the Arts and the Fence Trust.

*For my father and my brothers*

**I.**

When I was ten, I loved epilepsy. Or rather, I loved
Christine, my older brother's girlfriend.

I thought of her as *Chris* on fire, spending
all of her soft watts in her name.

I could set the word on fire because it was in italics.

The world was a faint inferno, a white nimbus
I saw around skulls.

This did not worry me more than anything else,

though I was impatient. People were burning. Couldn't
we hurry up?

The latest chanteuse lit her torch song in the radio
night after night,

her cough elegant & slow,

& my fourth grade teacher gave the class

so many scented stickers that we spent
a lot of time sniffing our books.

Like we were addicted to those calm, reasonable texts.

I kept praying to the maple outside
my bedroom window.

It was dying. I thought I could anoint it in some
vague fashion,

& it would work again.

I felt removed, like Chris when she'd forget her meds
& blur

from sleep to seizure,

& Duncan would send me away.

She got violent. She said things she never remembered.
They were secret.

They were essentially meaningless.

They seem sexy now. Like the arbitrary evolution
of *soul kiss* to *French kiss*.

She loved to spoon with us on the floor
in front of the fire, her in the middle.

I could not imagine

how Duncan felt about this. She had cheated on him
at his 15th birthday, with his best friend.

Often she would repeat her conditional wish
to me:

*If only you were older…*

She hid behind my body before I even knew it existed.

If I could reach back through the oil slick of the *I*,
through the triptychs & ellipses,

I'd say, *Look, I know that it is lovely & only just 1983,*
*but it's wrong to take this illness*

*as an offering.*

Every morning of senior year, your roommate ensures you awaken to the sound of Elvis grimacing over his guitar strings on the tape deck. He was sexy & contrite, & filled his pockets with kibble for hellhounds.

You get up from your bed as if from river mud & straighten your psychic string tie. Though you will be largely ignored, you are occult with fact behind the scorched creases of your prep school uniform. You can explain anything, except why you stumble back to your dorm bloodied from running through the woods.

Your roommate sighs & unscrews his computer for the gray ganglion of pot hidden behind the circuit board. For once, you spark up that treble clef of smoke & lie back on the ridiculous aqua comforter your mother gave you, holding your breath forever with runner's lungs. It is the only talent he envies you for.

In due course, you go off in ill-fitting tweed to classes where your nervousness makes you seem thoughtful: *So when you think about it… A Tale of Two Cities is really about being impotent. All right, maybe not totally.*

Long silences invariably follow, which you endure by staring out the window at a lawn so deeply green it looks botanically assassinated. Then the discussion resumes as if you had simply never spoken.

Insomnia means you spend a lot of time watching the wind on the moonlit soccer field make silvery math of the grass. You sense that someone—a person with no face—is waiting off-stage, ready to replace you.

This impersonal menace needs to be explained again to the benign x-ray of Cassiopeia, toward which your father says everything anyone has ever felt or spoken is traveling still, broadcast like the sadness of a vaudeville joke on a radio show.

Every night, just before you fall asleep, other voices start talking amongst themselves in the monochrome waters at the deep end of your brain. You try not to think about this too much, as there is nothing to be done that wouldn't involve medication.

Your thesis argues that the astral plane is a theme park for religious hallucinations, & your advisor lets you know the other faculty think you're somewhat *non-traditional* for a scholarship kid. Meaning, *surprisingly weird.*

None of the teachers appear to understand your paper at all, & the white Rastafarian student says they just don't get that you're kind of a mystic. He's wrong, of course, but it's sweet of him to say, so you take him up on his offer of recreational cough syrup before class.

Through the liquefied air, you hear your Classics teacher ask why Odysseus is so pissed, & you diagnose it as: *Too many muscles. Also, there's that other thing.* He's amused: *Oh? Just what would that be?* You shrug languidly. *The dead. They just don't fucking listen.*

You go shopping & make the mistake of buying a box of diminutive Twinkies because they are cheap. You eat four, then can't bear the sight of them.

Matt claims they stopped making new ones in 1978, & they start to resemble tan, spongiform tombs in which your spontaneous qualities are interred.

Jessica slips a note into the chapter on Augustine: *I don't suppose that I remembered to tell you that I find you infinitely intriguing?* She has not.

When she asks about your family, you say they run a lint collective in Provo, & she nods as if this is supposed to mean something. As if your calm demeanor was not ritually evoked each morning & clandestinely maintained throughout the day.

You are convinced that your classmates are secretly interesting & funny when you're not around. You never imagine that you might be profoundly disappointed by their inner lives. Then Jessica asks you to the prom. She's cute, & you feel merely penciled into the margins of the universe.

You share the neon silence of what she terms *the ambivalent limo,* but this reticence is nowhere in evidence afterwards in the kitchen of the convention hall. She cries on your shoulder & grimly finishes the last of the smuggled Asti.

Her mascara runs to tribal marks as she tells you her last boyfriend locked himself in the bathroom for three hours after their first time. *I wanted to be on top,* she says, *& I got, um, overly excited.*

You're not certain, but you would guess that most other people's evenings are not ending in tears. Outside the window, iced branches click emptily in the wind, & you do not kiss her champagne-slicked lips.

Instead, you mimic the dorm mother telling the two field hockey captains, *Break it up, folks,* when she caught them in bed stripped down to their moderately festive skirts.

She laughs. In other hotels throughout the city, some girls are crawling under beds to get away from their dates. Some are doing shots off Ouija boards. Some are trying to explain away the lightly stunned look of the very drunk. In here, you have done a good thing. You even suspect that you've gotten away with it.

Your advisor calls you out of lunch to his office to tell you gently that your uncle & his flight instructor ran out of gas & crashed their Piper Cub in an empty field.

Some minutes pass. You thank him for telling you, then take your glassy composure out into the red voltage of oak leaves drifting onto the streets. You are seventeen, & now he is only a word burning in dry grass.

You say calmly to no one, *This is probably going to hurt a lot later.* But it doesn't, & you don't know why. You become quite alert & write very small things in your diary with a great deal of precision.

The lacrosse star chases steroids with LSD & storms into your room to talk about geometry in an angry & unspecific way. During Parent's Weekend, he trashes his room when the acid unlocks a latent psychosis, which is loud, but not unexpected.

Twelve weeks pass, & your father sends you a desperately casual letter with blanks for you to fill in: *Are classes going well?* _____ *Enter correct address here:* _____ *Other things you would like to tell me about:* _____.

When you finally answer his calls, he asks what you've been doing, & you reply, *Thinking about the Sumerians*, because you don't want to seem lazy.

You meet Jessica at midnight in the smoking grove, but not to make out. Instead you sit on a fallen log, surrounded by the white, diacritical marks of used condoms, & tell her about your panic attacks.

You look up at the lit disaster map of Mare Imbrium, caring more about fixing those perfect errors than mastering the overwhelming feeling that you are grinding your own attractiveness into dust.

Jessica shrugs but is intent upon your silhouette. *You're afraid of... exactly...?* The grove looms in the half-finished light like the burned church of an idea, & your moon-occluded bodies seem to belong here.

She blurs the spent hexagram of cigarettes & latex with her sneaker as you explain in progressively smaller words how the fear is not so much a force as a way of inscribing the world with style.

She smiles gently. *You do know that this habit of being terrified & wise is going to be a little inconvenient, don't you? Like, if you plan to live past 30?*

She's right. Your job, as you saw it, was to be the one who watched—while immune—for the possibility of aurora borealis around each person who was in doubt. You liked it when they decided to be lined in that animate fire & forget who they were. To act, not be acted upon. As you should now.

—It's important to try to be practical about these things: see the apparition, then go back to sleep.

These are latter days. You regard the writ of frost on the window pane as a blueprint for something yet to come. Something severe & intricate.

Every few weeks, the drowned pilot from the bay walks up the stairs, dripping wet. But you go back to your bed over the furnace before he reaches the top—

Your sheets are stark parchment lit by a burning telegram that gives off the incense of human hair:

*It's still 1985, & your Mother is downstairs having sex with Hector & his cut-rate cocaine.*

When you tell this to your father you add, *Forsooth?*

Not everything about the medieval mind is witty, but you seem to think that it makes you approachable. It does not—

—In your father's filing cabinet, a short letter claims your IQ is !%!, & you wish you never found it.

It does not make the fifth grade any easier, & even though it seems like the last detail, you know there are more to come.

—He lowers his fall of blonde hair, taking his face away elaborately.

You love him because he suffers without excuse, unlike your older brother, who must ostentatiously starve himself with organic vegetables.

Duncan seems mauled by his spirit animals & just barely manages to be irritably serene.

He looks up from his radishes & kale & says that you must leave the house. He is going to channel The Bear now, & it is very loud—

Across the room, your younger brother relaxes into the hoarse declaratives from his relentless hardcore records.

The lead singers are averse to consonants & seem to feel that everything (mind, body, spirit, the world) has failed them—

—This seems neither New Age nor polite, but you have no choice.

The low afternoon light solders the sliding glass door into a slab of gold circuitry, & you step out cautiously into the aphasic shapes of the fallen snow.

—Your hair freezes, making you shiver like the prophetic children in the Brothers Grimm.

The art of staying alive when the story darkens with the dusk of plot depends on being boring.

Smirking as you eat the thorn apple.

Slipping into your twin's shadowy life.

Drinking the standing water to get to the stone at the bottom—

It's a lot of work, this sustained weirdness. You hope someone notices.

While you wait for the bus, you stare at the salt tablets grinding against one another mindlessly in the winter bay.

There's no conjunction that can be made of them—

—All around you, boys step out of the stories of their secret weekends smiling demurely like Venus & holding the smoke of testosterone against their bodies.

You listen carefully to them muttering lush from the drunken lake: *gooch, tripler, hebe...* slang that sounds communicative & friendly, but isn't.

—Consequently, you try to be so unruffled that people either find you boring or exotic. This has mixed results.

There are those who will hate you because you like to live in *Explanation*, that ideal, sinking city, its placid canals blind with beautiful data—

Your biology teacher alludes to aliens, pyramids, & auras, but seems to have a sense of humor.

So when he hands you a sharp glyph of crystals, you blurt out:

*My father used to be a clairvoyant & healer. That's what he did in Europe—*

—You look up. *Oh. Was that out loud?* It was.

You can see it on your teacher's face, as he thinks hard, trying to work around the black orchid growing more specific & lovely in his occipital lobe.

—He curses quietly, politely, & begins the failed print again, swaying obscurely in the Latinate odor of the chemicals.

You can only see the world clearly when it goes away.

The best time is during the odd, medicinal hours you spend with your father in his darkroom—

*It may seem dramatic, but really your soul chooses when you want to leave & whether to leave fast or leave slow.*

This is not how it works in your pulp novels. The hero gets drunk off the ache of the cub reporter's perfume. Then he grunts over a bullet & struggles not to say what he means—

—You don't know whether it's best to suffer invisibly, or, as your Irish aunt would say, *grandly.*

—All you can picture are Puritans crawling from the morally radioactive rubble of England.

It's a far cry from the cubes of communion bread & shot glasses of grape juice passed around at Church.

Your mother tells you sourly that the family is fallen Yankee aristocracy, & you smirk.

*Yeah*, you say, shaking your head, *that's a real bitch, all right*—

Your younger brother nods silently under the warped platelet of his hoodie. His stoicism makes you look like a hysteric.

All the same, it seems unfair that he just knows to reach under the front seat of Hector's Camaro for the grooved .38 hidden there—

—Hector laughs, says something diffident in Spanish, & places it back under the seat, presumably so that you won't be late to the matinee of *Supergirl*.

—While your mother is out buying a universe of avocado, you discover the .38 bandaged into a beige atom inside her panty hose.

You find the Bronze Age comforting & you dream about water polo players scowling outside their lockers as they chip obsidian blades one molecule wide—

Just perfect, you think, for brandishing at the butcher: *A full pound, damn it! & bloody!* The comedy makes you even sadder.

She's says she's holding it *for someone else.* You immediately tell your father about it when he picks you up for his weekend. It might be meant for him—

—He laughs. *Danger is relative. Sometimes, after a reading or a healing, I'd come to & be driving through a meadow at sixty miles an hour.*

*Spend too much time outside the body & you become like a paragraph, transitory & fictional.*

—If the "Narcs" catch you, you're tried before a jury of sixth graders.

But you are a star that week because you got off.

Your social studies teacher instructs the class on how to play *The Drug Game*.

Then he writes *1 drug* on slips of paper & passes them out secretly to all the "Pushers."

You're an "Addict" & get your drugs rolled up inside a borrowed ballpoint pen—

You excel at this game, mostly because what drives it doesn't exist & is worth nothing.

You prefer to traffic in abstractions. You learn the States on the floor in a semi-circle around the teacher's desk.

As the flashcard reveals each red outline, you rise off your heels & wave your hand insistently—

—Then you hear Sally whisper behind you: *All I can see is his sweet ass.*

You don't know it yet, but this will be the only time anyone ever openly sets aside your mind for your body.

—His poetry makes an argument you don't quite catch:

Your older brother sends you heavily-punctuated essays from the Sierras about how Kerouac should have died by lightning.

They arrive written in spirals on the outside of cardboard boxes filled with antiseptic tangles of evergreen branches—

*Sparrows perch on cattails…*
*No, wait! They're glued there!*

He's learned which plant will give you hypothermia.

It's upsetting to hear him like this. You prefer his explanation of why Southside Sulfur Jim fretted his guitar with a knife & dreaded the railroads.

But his instability is hip, an illness that lets him live in this world—

—Whereas you need pentagrams to go off every minute like cherry bombs just to illuminate how to avoid getting beat up.

Your younger brother shakes his head as he sorts his record collection by value.

*Just worry about your algebra, okay?*

Why can't your open secret
be a peroxide hologram
hidden in your locker?

Or a smudge of galactic
purple on your cheek? No
one wants to hear about
these things—

—But then your new friend
doesn't feel the need to
deflect the conversation to
the fleshy excesses of *Tramps*
or *Cherie* when you casually
allude to occultism.

He tells you over the phone
to lie back on your bed & he
will send some energy.

You look out at the sun firing
the grass into a jumble of
green exclamation points.
You feel nothing.

When you meet his parents,
you instantly recognize the
careful gestures of profound
depression.

You face squarely into the
solar wind that roars through
the quiet living room—

—It's refreshing, the lack
of emotional significance
attached to anything you
say. You might as well be
furniture.

As you help chop the
vegetables for dinner, the
mother mentions astral
projection as if it were a
method of self-help.

You regard the growing
pile of diced carrots fiercely:
*Really. I wouldn't know about
that.*

You pride yourself on your ability to make wry observations in terrible conditions.

Such as when Thanksgiving dinners devolve into shouting matches over whether or not someone had too much of the pearled onions—

—Your wisecracks don't solve anything, but they do pass the time when your mother & grandfather trade obscenities from 1956.

He thinks you are all weak & sentimental, ignorant of the incarnadine dollars pouring out of the wine bottle.

The only time you know what she's really thinking is during the fights. Or when she weeps bitterly over her failed fruit gelatins—

—You make yourself feel better by picturing her as a sci-fi housewife receiving the gray slag of her husband's remains.

This scene seems more comprehensible than the litany every holiday of how you & your brothers have ruined the past 20 years of her life.

Everything seems to go wrong in the world of the spirit just as much as in the world of matter.

However, the ineffable disappointments tend to be more profound & enduring—

—During his divorce vacation, your father bribes a guide to let him spend the night in the King's Chamber at Cheops.

He wakes up in the morning with a migraine from the five souls who still have to guard the tomb even though it was looted thousands of years before.

The stupidity of this psychic espionage is so impressive that you're overwhelmed by both skepticism & awe—

—At least you get to be amused by *Flash Gordon's* Ming the Merciless as he unintentionally sums up the hazards of the astral plain:

*Pathetic earthlings. Hurling your bodies into the void without an inkling of who or what is out here.*

Your older brother boasts that your father taught him how to move the ball of white light up & down his body—

—But this does not diminish the hours he spends in the fetid arcade, rocking back & forth over *Galaga*.

Your brooding friend Mike sneers at Pac-Man's *faggy pastel*, which you find confusing.

*That's Commie stuff*, he growls. *Like that goddamned Esperanto.*

You debate this further while browsing the black exoskeletons of the 300 toy guns in his shed, but don't get very far—

—This is, after all, a kid who shoots birds with BB rifles for fun & whose father keeps a grease gun stashed behind the radiator.

He is destined to be a cop, just as you are destined to be someone who is allergic to all forms of authority, especially your own.

—They were called *gentlemen's pistols* because they could fit easily in the pocket of a sport coat.

One night, your grandfather gets elegiac about bathtub gin & plays Scott Joplin on the piano.

Eventually, he digs out the jammed automatic he carried for arguing drunkenly with his inferiors in the rough parts of town—

Sentimentality is as close as he comes to being kind. The rest of the time, he seems to be enraged that no one wears spats any more.

You look over sextants in the antique shop & ask your father if this humanizes him at all.

He smiles. *Hard to say. Civic obligation was different back then.*

He staggers, clutches his arm, & then checks his pulse—

—When you go out to the alley, you discover that he's borrowed a derelict's heart attack.

You suspect that this intuitive information is not quite the blessing it's been made out to be.

You've been collecting Talmudic rebukes from the Zohar in order to irritate your astral projection friend.

But your father thinks you need to attend a cult support group meeting—

—On the way, you stop at a rest area, & your father wanders over to the gouged rock wall at the edge of the parking lot.

*My god. This is that Caponigro shot from 1959. This picture is the reason I got into photography.*

You examine the gray petrogylphs hacked into facets, the way the stone hurtles outward & inward. You float alone against its equations—

—When you were born & got sick, your father gave up teaching at Yale & running a gallery with another photographer, whom your mother hated because she was a lesbian.

Your failure to thrive is the least improbable thing that happened during your parents' marriage, which makes your almost-death feel quite mundane.

*—I myself got out in '78. I was sent to teach healing in Europe while my kids got scurvy from lack of fruit on the commune. I could see that my guru wasn't going to be able to keep it together.*

You can't breathe. You spread your hands flat on the cheap fold-out table.

True: the community came to grief for very good reasons. But that doesn't disprove the clairvoyance & the angel that appeared to him in the empty shower stall & told him what was needed to save your life.

You've never been able to understand why what moves you the most is not the data itself, but his warnings about the technology—

*—Every Mystery School, going back to Egypt & Atlantis, knows that everything is possible but not necessarily a good idea.*

*Even the* I-Ching *was a collection of spells before the Confucians purged it.*

*Some phenomena are pretty goddamned serious, & you can't always shut the door on them if you throw it open to the night.*

Other parents at the cult meeting talk about ritual hunger. About Sanskrit scribbled like the names of heavy metal bands across textbooks. Then your father clears his throat—

—Outside, the snow blisters the parking lot with its incidence. He tears open another nodule of sugar.

Your father sighs & empties a ziggurat of creamer into his diner coffee. *I quit because I got ahead of myself, so to speak.*

*I met my guide when I was out of my body. He did not approve of the energy work I was doing. He told me I was destroying my hippocampus—*

*To keep the higher centers of the brain open all the time wracks it to pieces.*

You understand. Every night you lie in bed & deliberately think your way outside the pale, aggregate universe.

Once you have spiraled out that far, it feels absurd that this language must or can represent being a thing that looks & has a before. It gives you a spiritual headache—

—You don't know it yet, but this is the opposite of orgasm: your sense of self dispersed into bloody radii, a luminous spatter set against a massive, dark velocity.

You always thought this vertigo just meant you were macabre in a scientific sort of way.

Your father looks over the arabesque of steam from his cup. *Anyway, it made me pretty uncomfortable to be able to see other people's thoughts.*

*Took five years to learn how to read minds, & another five to forget—*

—Your pulse aches in your cheeks. *What about my thoughts?*

He smiles. *I told you: I forgot how. But I kept just enough to know when people are lying to me.*

This terrifies you. You cannot unpack it all, & you resent how little difference education makes.

Even if you shut up about it, you will still be weird at the core.

Your father winces. *I'm not saying you have to ignore all this material. I don't. You couldn't if you tried—*

—*But the universe would much rather see a writer or a dancer or a painter than another prophet.*

*Those people aren't stuck with trying to figure out what it means when certain library books edge off the shelf & drop into their hands.*

There is no end point, no perfect, luminous principle. Your loved ones begin to curate their own absences.

The high-pressure system of acne moving across your face helps. You're grateful for the mild, pointillist flavor of the pain. It brings you back to yourself.

Your younger brother grimly reads anarchists who held grenades & adjectives in equal esteem.

Then he sorts bundles of pot furled into green dynamite.

*I love you, but I gotta blow this up. Can you take it outside?*—

—You take it all outside. You stare into the plutonian maze under the hood of your older brother's Ford.

It's depressing. He fusses over it like a siege engine. *Yuki paid for the transmission. It's no good. What a mistake that was to sleep with her.*

He is terribly attended. He blunders through rounds of spiritual retreats, confronting people until he is asked to leave.

He uses women, then drops them, blaming archetypes when they realize he will never be capable of holding down a regular job—

—The metaphors of alchemy, the dross & the gold, the ordinary & the sublime, eat him alive.

The vaporish tapes & New Age pamphlets do not help.

Eventually, everything you recognize as his, all the words that *are* him, spiral continuously out of his head like coriolis horns.

You want to speak up, to fix his grammar. But in the end it's just him & the bull on the tracks.

The black horns meeting his blue ones as he leaps off the train station edge.

## II.

I'd like to walk again in her weather, in the dark
through the fog,

its gray damage

laid down all over town.

When she couldn't bring herself to get up
from the bed, Belinda would say

it was like being

*the most stylish drowned person in the whole universe.*

It was the only likeness she allowed herself, besides
married women.

I asked her.

*Me? I'm the old word. What do you call it. A Sapphist.*

I think she liked to take them back from that kind
of touch. To smudge

the clear blueprints of oil from their breasts.

Her words were so wet the women took a long time
to notice how few of them she said.

For a year in college, I built myself into her silence.
It was so much effort

to even appear to be

interested in what anyone else was saying
that I thought

everyone could hear the splice

when the power died & the negatives unspooled
endlessly

on the black floor

below my brain.

Now, in this double darkness, I don't hate being
in the poem

or my body.

I can use my aesthetic expense account to underwrite
the hidden *z*

in *kismet* & *aphasia*.

Under each footfall, there's a penny on which someone
has scratched: *i hert*,

misspelling it so I won't get it wrong.

I can take everything away, become only a breath
with a lisp of salt, & no one—

not the speaker, not his stand-in—

can bring me back.

**III.**

I thought no one would ever surpass Jillian
when she came for two hours,

describing it afterwards simply as, *The universe
fucked me.*

It seemed awfully generous of it, & I was surprised,
since I had

assumed the universe could only climax
inside a sonata,

or a prime number

as long as your arm,

that true ecstasy was the pleasurable depression
of a Vermeer.

She didn't touch herself once—just held relatively still
on my bed

& screamed happily as the serotonin
seeped from her brain

& I watched from across the room

in the dark, somewhat afraid.

She was supposed to be guiding me on my first acid trip,
but her nervous system had other plans.

She said when I took the acid that I was
instantly considered

clinically insane,

though really I'd have forty minutes

before I'd see something unhealthy & stunning,
like a chromatic glimmer

around every noun.

Later she would also bloody her hand
against concrete

because it felt so good,

but that was just a special effect.

This was serious. This required breath control.

She was majoring in philosophy of music & had just
spent all semester

reading forty pages of Hegel

with a professor who spoke so slowly

we thought he had a very useful form of brain damage.

When she played Chopin, it made a blue ruin
inside my head, & I wanted

to breathe, *Here*

*it is written*, at the end of every measure, even though
it clearly wasn't.

That night, under full sail, she had to

kick the trunk of a mimosa tree & bellow at it
out of some

nameless need.

So it felt pointless every week

for our theory class to try to erase the forehead
of the sexless mannequin.

To imply that there were vast differences between

*the dear reader, you, & I*

& to pretend that a formula writ small on a piece
of blotter paper

& a very large & unfocused idea

couldn't make a girl scream.

**IV.**

When I first started writing, I liked to think in italics
whenever I was at a loss.

Not startled, but *terribly*

*surprised* or *caught unawares.* Then I could be
formally afraid.

Even the last summer when I'd gone into the woods
to figure out why I didn't

want to have sex with my parents' au pair, I knew

I was watching myself for the slant.

Then I found the shack with the Confederate flag
& the centerfolds

stapled apart

on oak trees & made insubstantial with bullets.

Weirdly-arched women with queasy smiles
interrupted by accompanying

paragraphs of *on top*,

*below, behind, before.*

As if prepositions could get you off.

It wasn't that I was going away to college. It was just
the room,

dominated by those crossed wrists & tasting of iron
& expectation.

It made me feel like I should ask for something.
A flat glass of water.

A kind word. That was it—it was sex

without words. It bothered me. Without direct address,
I couldn't

be sure I was really the one involved.

This made no sense. That year, words were not helping.

Whenever I heard one I thought was beautiful, I secretly
wrote it in the air

down by my side.

The calligraphy had to be absolutely correct, or
I'd have to

do it again. Up to thirty times.

Now I like the idea that there was always
an unbelievable word

hovering near my hipbone.

At the time, it was exhausting.

*Au pair* means treated "as an equal." Like family.

I knew I was in trouble when I liked the reference
more than the word:

*This foreign phrase has no exact English synonym*
*& not every American*

*knows what it means.*

I got it wrong.

**v.**

I still get it wrong. I thought the important part
was the room

where we lay in an overcast question,

but it was the poems Melanie wrote. The places
where she had to trail off.

In those days, I was little more

than centrifugal force & throwaway lines.

So I actually thought there might be an explanation
in her muffled line breaks,

in fifty words so spare you could stencil them
above a doorway

to stop the angel

from pausing. Which is to say: to make the angel go by.

Now when I brush her poems clean of hesitations,
I see that they were shored up

by Sapphic echoes—lyric endearments shipwrecked

in random places.

That's why I like to think that Sappho would have
loved her strangely,

being as dead as the numbers on dice.

& I'm not merely courting the indifference of a woman
who licked her last hypothetical

two thousand years ago.

I'm saying I love to get it wrong.

Perhaps the reason why I've been drawn to the direct
address all these years

is because you can talk to the beloved & the reader

without each one knowing

about the other.

## VI.

*There is this problem in writing*, my fiction professor
said, *of* utile & dulce:

*the useful & sweet.*

I would have liked it better if he'd been talking about
suicides.

Every time I enter the poem, I have to remind myself
that the brain

is not a damp, crystalline *Exit* sign. Only the dead

can drink what they want from the slipstream
of a sentence

& go out the same way they came in.

Always I think this will be the last room—Will's room,
the one

he rented for three days

before shooting himself.

The sheets glow with the ultraviolet light
of expired sperm,

a silkscreen of a gasp, the last corsage of sparks
before orgasm.

I'm sorry about that. Ideas won't even let us get
to the bed.

There's a small minus sign of cocaine on a mirror,
which he wanted

to try just once. *It seems so*

*fucking Platonic,* he told me, *like essence of sports car.*

I was afraid for him. Acid had taught me about
economics,

about diminishing returns.

For years I felt like a slightly imperfect
imitation of myself.

The only way to stop feeling like this was to consciously
rewire my brain

from the ground up.

This is an evasive way of saying that I had to think
myself back

from one type of brain damage

& toward another, more charming variety.
I concealed this

for more than a decade

until I thought no one could tell,

until the narrowing sentence of Will's secrets
revised itself

in that retroactive dark.

I've done it, of course. I can't help it. This is what
you do when you have access

to catastrophe: you change things.

Run the numbers one way

& his girlfriend felt a more subtle disorder in his cold
hands on her breasts.

Run them another way & the mirror is a changeable page
on which

is written something that is neither *yes* nor *no*,

a cryptic reason couched in a small caliber.

Run them all the way to the end, past the trembling
decimal holding back *pi*,

& we're wading

in Northrup Frye's cool excuse: *the poet makes no
specific statement of fact…*

*& is concerned not with what happened,
but with what happens.*

Will said it better: *Sometimes… you just wish you could
have sex*

*in the present tense.*

## VII.

You'll notice that I keep leaving things out. The articles, the antecedents

scrawled with anatomy.

It's not only because I'm afraid. When the people I love enter the ampersand,

they are changed.

Like music. *It is technically impossible,*

Rob tells me, *to play a minor chord on a guitar, because the echo in the air*

*makes it a major one.*

It was while Anne was playing Paganini's
*Moses Phantasie*

that I realized I would never

have sex with her.

Sex was a red harmonic line she thought she could never make straight

once someone troubled the waters.

Paganini used to weaken the strings of his violin so they'd snap

one by one

during a performance.

When he was finished, the music would never be
wrecked

quite that way again.

This is probably why even his enemies respected him.

I had been thinking of the Rubicon in Anne's mind,
the formal refusal

cut to let her look

into her body alone & without the mist of another's
anxiety over her reflection.

That was wise of her. There I was, worrying that
a headache's black opal

didn't belong in the subjunctive.

I'd spent a semester sounding out
sixteenth-century poets,

scanning the segmented lines

for each tinny accent.

Their bitterness & fidelity equally composed, lacquered
with such tact

that it made me want to spit.

Did they even deserve bodies? My dad shook his head.

*You have to remember: they felt like they had just
invented reasoned discourse.*

*They really needed it, because they were wading*
*through shit in the streets.*

He was right. Elizabethans specialized in the crux—
the loop of rhetorical music—

which is derived

from the *cross*, the *issue*, & the *insolvable problem*,
literally

*the torment (of interpreters).*

I envied the way Anne lived all at once, her misspellings
& mal-a-grams.

When I asked if she was going to change for work,
she'd lower

her eyes & smile. *No. I don't want to take off*
*my fedora.*

*It has mystic powers, you see.*

Even with logic or logos, I knew her fixed electricity
would never be

fully resolved on this

or any other page.

# VIII.

*Comparisons are odious*, the Catholics say, meaning,
*Metaphors in marriage*

*are hateful.*

    In Thomas Hardy's notebooks, he mentions the tactics
of English wives

chloroformed on their honeymoon beds, with notes
pinned

to their nightgowns: *Do with me what you will.*

    Such a reproach undoes exactly what it commands,
using grammar

to mop up the blood

in advance. The strength in sex

comes in odd places. On top of my bookshelf, I have
a Japanese soul doll made

from corn husks: a spindly, effaced woman

in withered robes the color of a calm flame.

    She is disaster uttered in ivory moiré, a female imago
that actually would

have made Richard III

*undertake the death of all the world.*

I bought it in Indiana, where the charnel house
of the corn fields

lay in state every fall, while I was dating a girl

whose brother, *the oxygen thief*, had taken her when
she was seven

& *inspected* her with his friends. Everything came down
to the verb.

I could tell

she was proud of her clinical precision.

Liz never swore, but she came more times
than I could count,

which made me

ashamed for counting. She lived

in minimalist Ohio, in an apartment complex blank
as a concussion, & I drove

three hours each way to see her every weekend,

as haunted by my PhD seminars as if I'd been
required to critique

the architecture of atomic particles.

*Yes, Erasmus was cunning. No, the martyrs did not have*
*sexually potent rhetoric. Yes, I thought*

*death was the definite article. Maybe.*

Then I'd return from feverish sex that made
time itself

strange & sluggish,

& wonder what I wanted.

Sex & the text may be compass points, but get too close
to the body & things

go awry, which is to say

they become inconvenient as things.

This is why I liked literature in the first place: because
the very last door

inside the image

was shut, & the lock fused

with a bloody ampersand:

*(the sign) by itself (means).*

## IX.

Yes. This is the last place, shaded by a vast
Decision Tree.

I can see the scars on the bark

where the branches have been torn away.

The word that burns my mouth is *cicatrix*.
I like it for the *x* alone.

I have never said it aloud, like most
of the words I know.

When I die, there will still be thousands

shrunk in their opalescence.

*Intimate* means *not having the power of speech*, which
should only apply

to animals, not poems,

or the humans powering them.

Every time I enter, the tree is different. This branch
grew from the first

pornographic magazine I hid

in the earth, from placing that hysterical text
below ground.

The tendency of living things is to become
more complex,

*to needlessly multiply possibilities or entities.*
So the snapshots

of duplicate pink

have complicated into chrysalis & stem.

The ground beneath the tree is lit by white orchids,
the waxy accidents

where animals spilled their seed.

The victims of the Permissive River congregate, sipping
from their cognates,

the extravagant waters

of those words *related by blood.* They are low & quiet,
a stylish murmur.

It's a homonym thing.

I must choose. On one side there are those
who hate their initials,

who have spoken for me

out of their small letters

& come & wept & remembered what
they put into their bodies,

& where all the etymologies are buried.

On the other, there are the dead, still dressed
in the static they emitted in life.

They have grubbed for Latin roots,

flickered back & forth between sexes

like film stars overlaid in monochrome cairns
on the cutting room floor.

Both have entered each stanza with their loves intact,
with the black pearls

of their obsessions setting off their eyes

& the hollows of their necks & wrists brushed
with concern.

I am terribly afraid they have become the same,
waiting for me.

They domesticate the orgasm with fact, illuminating
the 25 million spectral asterisks

that light up with each muffled groan.

They sterilize the trope with quotes, with Anita Bryant's
bewildering theory

of sexual essence:

*Homosexuals are the way they are because*

*the sperm they swallow is the most concentrated form*
*of life.*

I have almost forgotten who does what.

The resonance on either side of the denouement
is wrong, which is what keeps

the error ethereal, unable to die or live, like everyone
else here.

We have not all slept together, nor have we all
been changed,

as Paul wished.

But there is consolation in figures, in the event horizon,

in the wedding that won't:

The bride in the bathroom, vomiting because she took
too many painkillers

to smooth the evening out,

& the groom using a joint to wrap an acrid scarf
of amnesia around himself

in the rain blowing onto the porch.

& Will, the one who is no longer here, who is
dismantled into imagistic pixels,

sits on the edge of the stage with the bride's
eight-year-old daughter,

who is wiping glitter

from her cheekbones with the heels of her hands
as if a small miracle

had blown up in her face.

He is trying to explain the sophisticated nature
of the damage

that two people

can choose & why it all seems alike from the outside.

She is looking at him out of the multiplied light
near her eyes,

& he is transitioning, like weather, into the grace
of the past tense,

which is classy & composed, a style

subject to no argument

but its own.

## ACKNOWLEDGMENTS

Excerpts from *Ampersand Revisited* appeared in various publications, and are reprinted here with thanks: *Artful Dodge, Black Warrior Review, Blackbird, Chelsea, Construction Magazine, Crazyhorse, Hayden's Ferry Review, The Iowa Review, New World Writing, Notre Dame Review, Suss,* and *Western Humanities Review.*

This book would never have materialized without the formative pedagogical wrangling and patience of Cathy Bowman, Roger Mitchell, Maura Stanton, Scott Ward, Sterling Watson, David Wojahn, and Ray Wonder.

For invaluable help—both direct and indirect—with the consensual hallucination of authorship, I would like to thank Brittany Pipes Altimus, Piers Anthony, Andrea Baker, Mark Baxter, Dan Blask, Sara Cameron-Morley, Christopher Connors, Leo Demski, Margaret Flint, Michelle Flint, Timber Holmes, Michelle LaPlante, Leslie Anne Leasure, Brian Leung, Julie Madsen, Laurie Mead-McGrory, Rob Meyers, William Mintun, Alicia Mooney-Flynt, Jay Baron Nicorvo, Maryanne O'Hara, Mike Peluse, Alison Powell, Kara Rodgers, Margaret Ronda, Richard Siken, Graham Strouse, Anthony Tognazzini, Chris Tonelli, Kayoko Wakamatsu, G.C. Waldrep, and Doug Whidden.

A goodly chunk of these poems would not have been finished without the time afforded by the inestimable Rockport Collective and the delightfulness of their exquisite corpsae: Shauna Barbosa, Adriana Cloud, Heather Hughes, Abby Mumford, and Phoebe Sinclair.

For the other nerd universe, I would like to thank Jenn Espinoza, Alison Pierce, Bill Scott, David Scott, Marilyn Scott, and Nathan Scott. A hole is to dig, a molecule is to bond, an RPG is to play.

Language fails me in trying to describe the depth of the debt I owe to the readers and editors of this manuscript in its many iterations: Rob Arnold, Rebecca Black, Eleanor Boudreau, Elisa Gabbert, Heather Hughes, Cecily Iddings, Heather Madden, Phil Metres, Justin Petropoulos, Elise Scott, Julia Story, Brian Teare, and Fritz Ward. Any unfortunate lacunae are mine, not theirs, and the world of ideas would be a much bleaker place without their elegantly liminal sensibilities and brains.

Similarly, I could not imagine living without the love and support of my family: Brian Berry, Cari Berry, Elena Berry, Jennifer Berry, Joshua Berry, Susana Raquel Berry, Cordelia Clark, Jacqui Grimwade, and Nancy Janus.

Thank you, Ariana Reines, for bestowing this fabulous honor on my recursive conjunction, and thank you, Rebecca Wolff, for curating the wonderful textual home that is Fence Books, and for setting aside a place in its illustrious catalogue. Thanks to Jess Puglisi for a lovely design and to Paul Caponigro for the generous use of his image.

Many thanks to the organizations that supported the writing of these poems: the Dana Award, the National Society of Arts and Letters, the Massachusetts Cultural Council, the Academy of American Poets, and the Ford Foundation. Special thanks to Stephanie Stio and the editors and funders of the National Poetry Series for keeping this magnificent opportunity alive.

## PERMISSIONS

"Pathetic earthlings. Hurling your bodies into the void..."
Lorenzo Semple, Jr., *Flash Gordon*, Universal Studios (Starling Films, Inc.)

"the poet makes no specific statement of fact..."
Northrop Frye, *Educated Imagination and Other Writings on Critical Theory, 1933-1962*, University of Toronto Press, 1996

## ABOUT THE AUTHOR

SIMEON BERRY has been an Associate Editor for *Ploughshares*, and won a Massachusetts Cultural Council Individual Artist Grant and a Career Chapter Award from the National Society of Arts and Letters. His work has appeared in *Crazyhorse, AGNI, Colorado Review, Blackbird, DIAGRAM, The Iowa Review, American Letters & Commentary*, and many other journals. His second book, *Monograph*, won the 2014 National Poetry Series (University of Georgia Press). He lives in Somerville, Massachusetts.

# FENCE BOOKS

## OTTOLINE PRIZE

| | |
|---|---|
| *Inter Arma* | LAUREN SHUFRAN |

## MOTHERWELL & ALBERTA PRIZE

| | |
|---|---|
| *Negro League Baseball* | HARMONY HOLIDAY |
| *living must bury* | JOSIE SIGLER |
| *Aim Straight at the Fountain and Press Vaporize* | ELIZABETH MARIE YOUNG |
| *Unspoiled Air* | KAISA ULLSVIK MILLER |
| *The Cow* | ARIANA REINES |
| *Practice, Restraint* | LAURA SIMS |
| *A Magic Book* | SASHA STEENSEN |
| *Sky Girl* | ROSEMARY GRIGGS |
| *The Real Moon of Poetry and Other Poems* | TINA BROWN CELONA |
| *Zirconia* | CHELSEY MINNIS |

## FENCE MODERN POETS SERIES

| | |
|---|---|
| *My Not-My Soldier* | JENNIFER MACKENZIE |
| *In the Laurels, Caught* | LEE ANN BROWN |
| *Eyelid Lick* | DONALD DUNBAR |
| *Nick Demske* | NICK DEMSKE |
| *Duties of an English Foreign Secretary* | MACGREGOR CARD |
| *Star in the Eye* | JAMES SHEA |
| *Structure of the Embryonic Rat Brain* | CHRISTOPHER JANKE |
| *The Stupefying Flashbulbs* | DANIEL BRENNER |
| *Povel* | GERALDINE KIM |
| *The Opening Question* | PRAGEETA SHARMA |
| *Apprehend* | ELIZABETH ROBINSON |
| *The Red Bird* | JOYELLE MCSWEENEY |

## FENCE MODERN PRIZE IN PROSE

*McGlue*                                    OTTESSA MOSHFEGH

## NATIONAL POETRY SERIES

*Ampersand Revisited*                       SIMEON BERRY
*The Meatgirl Whatever*                      KRISTIN HATCH
*Your Invitation to a Modest Breakfast*      HANNAH GAMBLE
*A Map Predetermined and Chance*             LAURA WETHERINGTON
*The Network*                                JENA OSMAN
*The Black Automaton*                        DOUGLAS KEARNEY
*Collapsible Poetics Theater*                RODRIGO TOSCANO

## ANTHOLOGIES & CRITICAL WORKS

*The Racial Imaginary: Writers on Race*      CLAUDIA RANKINE,
*in the Life of the Mind*                    BETH LOFFREDA &
                                             MAX KING CAP, EDITORS

*Not for Mothers Only: Contemporary Poets on*   CATHERINE WAGNER &
*Child-Getting & Child-Rearing*                 REBECCA WOLFF, EDITORS

*A Best of Fence: The First Nine Years,*      REBECCA WOLFF &
*Volumes 1 & 2*                              FENCE EDITORS, EDITORS

## POETRY

*Sleeper Hold*                               JIBADE–KHALIL HUFFMAN
*Cold Genius*                                AARON KUNIN
*The Lost Novel*                             JAMES SHEA
*my god is this a man*                       LAURA SIMS
*House of Deer*                              SASHA STEENSEN
*Colony Collapse Metaphor*                   PHILIP JENKS
*Undergloom*                                 PRAGEETA SHARMA
*A Book Beginning What and Ending Away*      CLARK COOLIDGE

## FICTION

FENCE
BOOKS